Making Independence Happen, One Paw at a Time

**The Story of Team Chally, Service Dog Ambassadors
for Canine Companions for Independence**

Amy Chally and Yazzen Chally

3 1257 02564 6844

ISBN-13: 9781519135377
ISBN-10: 1519135378
Library of Congress Control Number: 2015919021
CreateSpace Independent Publishing Platform
North Charleston, South Carolina

TABLE OF CONTENTS

DEDICATION

I'd like to dedicate this book to God; my family; my boy, Yazzen; and my Canine Companions family. To my family, thank you for your love and support. I would not be where I am today without you. To Lisa and Harold, Yazzen's puppy raisers, thank you for doing such a good job raising and training him during the first year of his life. To Canine Companions, thank you for giving me such a great dog and for setting me on my path to a more independent life. To my boy, Yazzen, thank you for giving me more independence and for making my life better every day you were with me.

ACKNOWLEDGMENTS

I'd like to thank my friend and fellow author Kelsey Browning and my CreateSpace team for their help with turning my passion project into reality. Kelsey, your support and your talent as an author have been invaluable throughout this entire process. Thank you for being so giving of your time and your talent, and for your willingness to share your thoughts and ideas to make me a better writer. I'd also like to thank my photographer's Charles Burhan and Lindsay Venturini for their beautiful photos on the front and back cover.

ABOUT THE AUTHORS

Hi! I'm Amy, a thirty-four-year-old licensed social worker with spastic quadriplegia cerebral palsy, a condition caused by trauma to the brain, usually during or shortly after birth. All four of my limbs are affected by this condition, and because of high muscle tone (muscles that are constantly tight and contracted), I struggle to move and control the muscles in my arms and legs. As a result, my limbs are often stiff, and they don't always do what I want them to do. I can walk with a walker, but I utilize a power chair and a service dog for independence and mobility in my daily life.

Hi! I'm Yazzen, a black Labrador–golden retriever crossbreed, trained by Canine Companions for Independence and the first member of Team Chally. As her service dog, I was trained to help Amy increase her independence while reducing her reliance on others. Amy and I worked and played together from July 31, 2005 until July 7, 2014. This is our story, divided into two parts. Part one is my story, from the time I was born to my life with Amy. Part two is Amy's story about her choice to get an assistance dog and how she chooses to delight in diversity and defy her disability. I hope you learn a few things from reading both stories. First, I hope you learn how dogs like me help individuals with physical challenges and enrich their lives. Second, I hope you learn that people who are dealing with differences are not much different from you.

MY QUEST FOR A LIFE WITH A PURPOSE

My life was planned for me before it even began. My parents, Elodie and Hanford II, were breeders for Canine Companions for Independence (CCI). CCI is an organization that provides highly trained assistance dogs, free of charge, to children, adults, and veterans with disabilities, including but not limited to cerebral palsy, autism, and Down syndrome. CCI does not receive any government funding to cover the cost of training us, and it costs $45,000 to train and place just one dog. The organization breeds Labrador retrievers, golden retrievers, and crosses of the two breeds. They train their puppies as facility dogs, hearing dogs, skilled companion dogs, or service dogs, depending on the needs of the applicant.[1]

As breeders, my parents' job was to bring puppies into the world, with the hope that those puppies would help others live more independent lives. My siblings—Yassy, Yvette, Yeena, Yoki II, Yakime, Yuma, Yolie, Yogi II—and I were born on November 23, 2003, in Silicon Valley, California.

Every CCI litter is assigned a letter of the alphabet and given names that are short and easy to say, but are very different from the commands we may learn. For instance, a CCI dog could never be named "Doug," because "Doug" is too similar to "tug." Even though my name is relatively short, people always misunderstand Amy when she says it, so she often has to spell it. The names can be chosen by the breeder caretakers, the general public, or by CCI, but the

---

1 Author's note: Facility dogs are dogs partnered with handlers that work in various settings, such as courts, schools, or hospitals. Hearing dogs are partnered with deaf or hard-of-hearing persons who need to be alerted to specific sounds. Skilled companion and service dogs are discussed in Amy's Story.

organization has the final say on all the litter names. You may be wondering how I got my name. I can tell you that CCI most likely named me after someone with the last name of Yazzen who donated to the cause (Larin and Cortez 2013).

We were the Y litter, my mom's fifth and final litter before she stopped working for CCI. We were born at her home and lived there with her and her (breeder caretaker) family until we were eight weeks old. Then her family had the difficult job of taking us back to CCI's national headquarters in Santa Rosa, California, and saying good-bye.

SHEPHERDING THE LITTER

We missed our mom and her family, but being back at CCI's headquarters meant the second stage of our quest to become assistance dogs was about to begin. In this stage, we went from CCI's headquarters to one of CCI's five regional centers. From there, we were paired with different volunteer puppy raisers, who might live in different states within the region. So for my siblings and me, this meant we would no longer be together. In fact, we were sent all over the country, with my sisters Yeena and Yoki II in the southwest region, my sister Yakime and brother Yuma in the southeast region, my brother Yolie and sisters Yassy and Yvette in the northwest region, and my brother Yogi II and me in the north central region.

I lived with my puppy raisers, Harold and Lisa O'Connell. Living with them was great! They were in charge of making sure I was safe, well cared for, and ready to become an assistance dog. They puppy-proofed their house and lawn and provided me with food, health care, and socialization opportunities at their expense. They took me to work, church, doctor's visits, and other places to give me the chance to interact with people and explore new environments. Together we attended CCI-approved obedience classes where, under their watchful eye, I learned my name as well as commands including sit, down, shake, stay, and up.

In addition to teaching me my name and the commands, Harold and Lisa sent CCI monthly progress reports. These reports stated whether or not I was staying healthy, responding to my commands, and exhibiting appropriate behavior when exposed to people, places, or things. My progress reports showed that I did not have any major problems learning my commands or behaving appropriately. If anything, I performed too well, and I liked being the center of attention.

I recall one day, when my neighbor's ducks waddled into the yard, I really wanted to play with my new feathered friends, but Lisa asked me to sit. Through our training, I learned that "sit" meant that I was to place my butt on the ground while resisting the urge to move. So I stayed still and stared, and instead of playing with them, I performed for them. As they got closer to me, I showed them the best sit, stand, and down I possibly could (O'Connell 2012).

People with my name or variations of it have "a desire to please, be appreciated, admired, and perfect; they are required to do a good job at everything they do" (First-Names-Meanings; Baby Names Numerology 2014). I loved showing my skills to anyone or anything that would watch. The more we practiced my commands and socialization, the better I got. The more skilled I became at my commands, the more I wanted to work and do what Lisa and Harold asked of me. We were a team, and we worked very hard so that someday I could become an assistance dog.

When I was a year and three months old, my someday came, and as much as Harold and Lisa wanted me to stay with them, their desire to see me succeed was stronger. So they put aside their wishes and took me back to CCI's north central training facility in Delaware, Ohio, where they said good-bye. All they could do now was wait and hope. Hope that my first two weeks back at the center would go smoothly. Hope that all my X-rays, medical exams, and temperament/behavior tests would show that I was healthy and not overly excited, fearful, or easily distracted. In these first two weeks, if the trainers felt I wasn't healthy or didn't have the right temperament or character traits to become an assistance dog, I would be released from the program and go back home to Harold and Lisa and live my life as their pet.

MAKING THE GRADE

Luckily, I did not have any medical or temperamental problems, so I continued with advanced training, the third stage of my quest to become an assistance dog.

In the first three months of advanced training, the trainers built upon the groundwork of my puppy raisers. I learned how to work around a wheelchair and retrieve dropped items. During this stage, the trainers would also use a rabbit and cats they had at the center to desensitize my prey drive. Learning how to perform these new tasks and behave around these animals was hard work. However, I knew I had a job to do, and I wanted to do it well. As much as I wanted to be back home with Harold and Lisa, I wanted to make them proud of me even more!

I had no idea my new trainers were testing me at various points during my three-month stay. However, I must have impressed them with my work ethic and ability to perform the commands my puppy raisers had taught me, as well as the new tasks I was learning. They gave me a passing grade and decided to keep me at the center for three more months of training.

During this time, I learned more than forty commands. The really difficult work began at this stage. I had to continue practicing the skills I already had learned in addition to learning how to perform new commands, such as turning a light on or off and tugging open doors and pushing them shut. I also had to prove that I could ignore distractions such as squirrels and rabbits, and perform these tasks outside the comfort of the training center. If I could stay on task no matter where I was, I knew I would meet my life partner…or would I?

THE BOY IN BLUE

So far I had worked my tail off in advanced training, doing my best to prove I could be a CCI assistance dog. There was only one thing left for me to do, and that was to earn my blue vest for good and meet my match: a child, adult, or a veteran with a disability, or a professional who works with these individuals. I had waited a long time for this moment, but so had the recipients waiting to receive one of us. CCI requires every person who needs an assistance dog to complete an application. During this time, applicants must complete paperwork, answer questions over the phone, and travel to their regional center to answer questions in person. This entire process can take three to six months, but once a person's application is complete, they're accepted into the program and put on the wait list for team training. Then the potential recipient must wait for the phone call inviting them to attend team training at the appropriate regional center. A recipient may wait for their team training call anywhere from six months to two and a half years, or even longer. Team training lasts two weeks and is scheduled for six days a week, eight hours a day. During this time, potential handlers learn how to care for us and how to use the forty-five commands we already know, which will help them become more independent.

In the north central summer team training class of 2005, there were only seven people who needed a dog. Therefore, if I wanted to make it as an assistance dog, I could not slack off. I had to keep performing well. I remember being very anxious those first few days as I waited to find out whom I was matched with and what my role would be. On the third day of team training, the long wait was over. I was going to be a service dog partnered with Amy, a young woman with spastic quadriplegia cerebral palsy (CP). She would use me to help her be more independent in her day-to-day life. I would help her pick up and carry items, pull open doors and push them shut, and more!

Just for fun, CCI gave every participant the chance to list the top three dogs they hoped to be matched with. I didn't know it at the time, but I wasn't Amy's first choice; I was her third. When Amy realized I was her dog, she was nervous, and she wondered what the trainers were thinking, because as you'll find out, I was so stubborn. I, too, had my doubts. Even though Amy and I were matched on the third day of training and together all the time, I was so nervous that my tail would not wag. Amy and her mom often joked that they were going to buy me a shirt that said, "Stop looking at my tail!"

I knew I had to calm my nerves and start changing the way I was responding to Amy. If the trainers did not like what they were seeing, there was a chance they wouldn't place me with her. She deserved a chance at a more independent life, but being matched with Amy did not guarantee our success in the program or that our placement would be permanent. If at any point during training the trainers felt like Amy couldn't perform her duties as a handler, the placement would not be made. Similarly, dogs that didn't perform well with their first match could be placed with another person, held back until the next team training session, or the least favorable option: released from the program completely.

CCI can release a dog from the program at any point in the process, though it is rare for the organization to do so during team training. Because of its high standards and expectations of the dogs in the program, CCI's placement rate is only 40 to 60 percent (Fatka 2012). So I wanted to do the very best I could to help Amy and go to my forever home.

Team training was a lot of hard work, but it was also fun. Amy had homework and tests every night based on the daily lectures, which covered the topics of leadership skills, canine behavior psychology, and canine learning. I eventually relaxed and became so comfortable in my role as a service dog that I'd moan loudly during the lectures because I was so bored and so eager to work. You see, people with my name or variations of it "hate to sit still for too long. We are very active; we love to travel, try new things, and take chances" (Birth Village 2014). This may explain why I preferred to be doing the fun stuff like taking field trips and practicing my working commands in our team training sessions. I remember one training session where we ran relay races with the four basic food groups. One of the items we had to carry in our mouths, without breaking, was a raw egg. The only time one broke was during a human-to-human transfer!

In team training, our handlers learned the importance of leadership, patience, persistence, laughter, support, and encouragement. If things weren't going right with a particular command for what seemed like the umpteenth time, the whole class would help motivate the dogs. Classmates and trainers would all say, "That's it," to let the dogs and handlers know they were on the right track. Amy felt that support when I refused to turn on a light, something I had done countless times in advanced training without a problem. During this moment of resistance, Amy found herself wondering just how hard she could chin-bop me. A chin-bop is a correction where Amy would gently "bop" me in the hollow spot on my chin. Luckily, she didn't have to use it, and when I finally turned on the light for her that day, there was a huge celebration. Every handler quickly learned that a game of fetch or a scratch behind the ear for a job well done would get them far when motivating us and helping us keep our desire to work.

Amy and I had come a long way during our two weeks at team training, and we were well on our way to becoming a team—Team Chally! There was only one hurdle left for us to pass: the public access test. Amy was really nervous about this final test before graduation, but I knew we had it in the bag. All we had to do was show the trainers we could function as a team in public. For us, this meant Amy had to show how well she could give me a series of commands, and I had to show how well I could carry out those commands while in a public place.

During the test, everything was going great! I was following through with every command Amy was giving me and we were completing each task without a problem. Then the unthinkable happened. Just as Amy told me to get a pen she had dropped on the floor, someone petted me without asking. In the service-dog world, "drive-by pets"—as we affectionately call them—are a no-no because they can distract me from my work, in this case, picking up the pen. Amy did not know what to do because if she had told the individual "no," "don't," or "stop" and I had heard her, I would've stopped picking up the pen. Because in our world, "no," "don't," and "stop" are commands Amy can use to make a particular behavior I'm doing cease. Luckily for us both, I did what any good service dog should do. I ignored the petting and continued working, and we passed the public access test. By law, I could now go anywhere with Amy for the next six weeks.

Now all we had left to do was graduate! Graduation was great! Before the ceremony, our class had to sit through one final lecture, and then I got to have some one-on-one time with my puppy raisers, who were invited by CCI to see us graduate and to participate during a pivotal point in the ceremony. It was so nice to be with Harold and Lisa again. I found myself turning back into a puppy, and I was thoroughly enjoying playing and cuddling with them, but soon it would be time for the three of us to reunite with Amy for lunch. During this time, Amy, Harold, and Lisa got to know each other and Amy got to ask them questions about what I was like as a puppy. After lunch, it was time to get down to the business of graduating. During the ceremony, people who weren't at team training got to see a little of what we experienced. They watched a high-light reel and listened to a speech given by a classmate who talked about the lessons we learned and the friendships we made. After the video and speech, and the presentation of a new class of puppies into advanced training, it was time for the presentation of the leash. During this very emotional part of the ceremony, Lisa handed my leash over to Amy, presenting me to her. After the presentation of the leash, graduation was over, the final stage of my quest to become an assistance dog was complete, and it was time to say our good-byes to Harold and Lisa, our friends, and our trainers before heading for my new home in the western suburbs of Chicago, Illinois.

LIFE WITH MY FOREVER FAMILY

I wish I could tell you that after the long drive home from Ohio, we were able to take a vacation from Amy's life to get to know each other better, but we only had a day. The next morning Amy and I had to report to her classes at Aurora University, where we would spend the next year of our lives as she finished her degree in social work. I will never forget the first day I went to college with Amy. It was exciting and a little nerve-racking. I just hoped I could do everything she needed me to do. I can remember the first time I had to help her open the bathroom door; I was so nervous that I wouldn't be able to do it. But my nervousness quickly turned to excitement because I opened the door, accomplished my task, and made her so happy.

With me by her side, Amy developed a confidence she didn't have before. She now knew I would be able to help her pick up dropped items and pull or push open doors, reducing her reliance on other people to perform those tasks for her. I also helped her make friends and score brownie points with many of her classmates. My habit of moaning loudly out of sheer boredom during lectures would get them out of class early because the professors would take pity on me.

Amy and I adjusted well to our new life together, and we really began coming together as a team. Before we knew it, six weeks had passed, and we were headed to see the trainers again for another public access recertification test. This time, Amy was not as nervous about it because she knew what to expect and had confidence in our abilities as a team. As expected, we passed our recertification, which meant that from now on we would only have to re-certify every two to three years.

With that out of the way, Amy and I focused on continuing to build our relationship as a team. At home and college, we continued practicing the commands we already knew, and Amy was also teaching me new ways to help her. For example, at home I was learning how to get the phone and the television remote from various places and bring them to wherever she needed them. For safety's sake, Amy also taught me how to get her seatbelt for her when it fell beyond her reach. I also learned and perfected how to help Amy transfer out of her couch with the footrest up. I accomplished this by putting my front paws up on the footrest and pushing it down out of her way. I learned this skill after only two days of practice.

Something interesting to note about my life is that when we worked at home, I didn't need to wear my vest. Wearing my vest wasn't a requirement for me to perform my work, but it let the public know I was working. At college, we continued to work on pulling open doors and picking up dropped items. When Amy didn't need me, I did my very best to become invisible, only giving the occasional moan.

Amy and I graduated from Aurora University in May of 2006. After being unemployed for a few months, Amy decided we would go back to Aurora University to earn her Type 73 professional educator license, which would allow her to practice social work in the schools. She received her PEL in July of 2007.

So in August of 2008, we embarked on yet another journey together when Amy took her first job as an elementary school social worker. By this time, it was clear that we made a great team. I loved going to work with her, especially during her first year, because we interacted with students all day and I still got to help Amy if she dropped something, needed a door opened, or needed an extra paw to carry things. I also spent a lot of time playing with my new friend Magnus, the Life Skills Program class rabbit.[2] Even though it had been years since I had been around one in an enclosed space, I fell hard for my new friend and found myself giving him kisses!

---

2 Author's note: According to Amy, the Life Skills Program is a program that teaches public school students with severe disabilities how to perform daily living and job-related activities.

The next six years brought some unexpected changes. In June 2010, Amy faced unemployment for the second time when the special education cooperative she worked for went through a reduction in force. Then, in July 2013, she faced the realization that I might not be able to work for her much longer. During my annual physical, the vet found a mast cell tumor on the right side of my chest—it was cancer. A day after my diagnosis I went back to the vet clinic to undergo a lumpectomy. The prognosis after my surgery was good. The vet was able to remove all traces of cancer, and no further treatment was necessary. A few weeks later, I returned to work helping Amy at home with no restrictions. It felt good to be working again and by October 2013, Amy became employed again. She began working for a Center for Independent Living, and I was right there by her side to help her pick up things she dropped, pull open doors, or do anything else she asked me to do.

In the nearly nine years since we first became partners, one thing remained the same, my love of working with and caring for Amy. It was clear that we function best as partners, and we make each other better. Without me, Amy was not as independent, and without her, I was just a well-trained dog with nothing to do but be a dog.

Not that there is anything wrong with being a dog. And Amy was really good at making sure that I got the chance to play fetch or lounge in my pool during the summer. However, whenever we'd play, she had to restrict the number of throws I was allowed to fetch because her arm would wear out way before I would! But playing fetch wasn't the only time I got to be a dog. I became a dog again any time Amy and her parents left the house without me.

Due to rights given to us by the Americans with Disabilities Act (ADA), I could go anywhere with Amy, but there were places she chose not to take me. For instance, I hardly ever went to physical therapy with her because I couldn't be under her control there. And when she ate at restaurants, visited family, or went on vacation with her parents or her friends, then most of the time I didn't go because they were there to help her.

Therefore, when Amy and her parents left the house without me, I lost all sense of self-control and helped myself to my brothers' food if their bowls were left on the floor. My brother Tai was a brown and white shih tzu, and my brother Koda was a black and gray shih apso (a shih tzu-Lhasa apso) mix. They were little lap dogs, and Amy thought they looked like Ewoks with fluffy curli-cue tails, only cuter. Their food wasn't the only thing I helped myself to when I was left alone with my ideas and rules. I also got comfy in Amy's bed or on the couches in the living room, all of which wasn't allowed. But when the cats were away, this dog would play. People with my name or variations of it do not like being left behind, and I was no different. When it looked like Amy and her fam-ily were getting ready to go somewhere without me, I'd get up and go toward the door, staring at them with my sad, guilt-inducing eyes.

Although I didn't always get to go along, Amy knew I was open to new experiences, including road trips and flights, and I was allowed to go on my fair share of both. During my first flight in the spring of 2009, I quickly learned I had to get used to the sights, sounds, and smells of the airport; the routine of the security check; and the apprehension of the takeoff and landing. If I could do that, Amy knew the rest would be easy. Since she got to board first, we had the seat in the front of the plane, which meant there was plenty of space for me to lie at her feet. I was a rock star; I didn't have any accidents, and I didn't need my chew toy as a distraction. In fact, I was able to relax enough to take a nap going to and coming from Texas.

The trip itself was great! I saw the rest of Amy's family and some points of interest like the San Antonio River Walk. At the River Walk, I took my first boat ride and had my first nerve-racking encounter with a revolving door that I could not figure out how to walk through. Amy describes it as a spinning merry-go-round with doors. I had never seen anything like this, not even in training, and now I had to prepare to walk through it! I was so nervous, but I tentatively put one foot in front of the other and followed Amy's lead. She had me sit while we waited to walk through the doors. I don't know what I was so nervous about, because I handled that situation like a pro! We also visited the Alamo and a wildflower park, where I posed with a scorpion, not a real one but a big brass one. I guess what Amy says is true: everything is bigger in Texas—even the lawn sculptures! I also got to take time off to play with Elway, a Texas blue lacy whom I met on one of our last days there. We had such fun chasing each other.

Although I loved to be a dog, I knew my place was with Amy. I was always happiest when I was with her. Ready, willing, and able, I was always there to do my share of work. I became alert if I heard something drop, hoping Amy would give me the "get" command. However, now and then, someone else would jump in to provide unsolicited help when Amy had given me a command. When this happened, I sometimes gave them a look that said, "What do you think you are doing? That's my job."

Perseverant and stubborn, once I set my mind on something, I didn't give up easily because I felt required to do a good job, and I had a need to please. Sometimes, I became confused about what Amy wanted, so I'd bring her anything I could get my mouth on because I wanted to make her happy. On the off chance that I was unable to perform a task, like pulling open a heavy door, I'd become very sad and disappointed in myself. I hung my head and dropped my tail between my legs, and it took a lot of hugs and pets from Amy to pull me out of my funk. Even though I felt sad when I couldn't perform for her, deep down I knew she was happy with me as long as I tried my best to do the things she asked of me.

Although I could share a story from every day of my life with Amy, I also want Amy to have a chance to chat with you. She's such a special person who has much to share about her life and the lessons she's learned. After you read her story, you'll understand better how I changed her life. But most importantly, I hope you learn how courage, faith, and love help Amy get through the obstacles she faces in life.

AMY'S STORY

EXPLORING THE PROSPECT OF
A MORE INDEPENDENT LIFE

Thanks, Yazzen. I do have a lot to share, but before I talk about defying disability and delighting in diversity, I want to share more about how I learned about Canine Companions and how I eventually decided I was ready for a more independent life.

I couldn't have been more than thirteen years old when I first heard about CCI. My parents and I were at the Abilities Expo—a huge exhibition for service providers and product vendors who work with persons with disabilities. I am a huge dog lover, so when we walked past CCI's booth and I saw the cute little puppies they had with them, naturally I had to stop and see what they were about. Once the trainers placed a little puppy named Bianca in my lap and she began snuggling and loving on me, I was hooked! I was also very intrigued by the idea that a dog could increase my independence. I was ready to fill out an application there and then, but my parents weren't ready to sign on the dotted line. They wanted me to get older and more mature before we considered getting another dog—especially an assistance dog.

When I turned seventeen, we began to seriously consider applying for an assistance dog. I never forgot what I had learned that day we met Bianca, and as we started to research service dog organizations, we liked that CCI never put a dollar amount on a person's need for an assistance dog. Other organizations we researched said that the more money we were able to give to their organization, the higher my priority and position on their waitlist would be. The subject of money never came up with CCI, and so after more research, we ultimately decided CCI was the right organization for our family and me.[3]

CCI will place dogs with recipients of any age. However, if a person who needs a dog is unable to command and control it without the use of a facilitator, someone who helps a recipient command and control the dog, then these individuals would apply for a skilled companion. However, if a person who needs a dog is eighteen and can control and command the dog independently without the use of a facilitator, then s/he would apply for a service dog. Both types of dogs reduce a person's reliance on other people to perform activities of daily living tasks, and both types of dog act as buffers to enhance social interaction. My parents and I were pretty sure that I wouldn't have any difficulty commanding or controlling a dog independently, so we waited until I turned eighteen before we began the application process so that I wouldn't need to use a facilitator.

On December 27, 1999, I applied for my service dog. Then on July 11, 2000, at the age of nineteen, exactly six months after I applied, I was accepted into the program and put on the waitlist for team training. Unfortunately, I was on the waitlist for more than two years. I have never been very patient, and meeting the dogs during the personal interview and seeing firsthand what they could do for my life made waiting very difficult. So when I received the call to come to team training in November 2004, but I couldn't go because I had to stay and take my college finals, I was very disappointed. I didn't know how much longer I could wait. Luckily, I didn't have to wait long, and on July 31, 2005, five years after they put me on the waitlist, I was about to start my first day of team training with my mom by my side as my training assistant.

Team training was a lot of hard work and fun. So much fun that when it was time to graduate, I felt a swirl of different emotions: happiness, excitement, trepidation, and sadness. I was happy and excited because Yazzen was finally

---

3 Author's note: If you are in need of a service dog, or know someone who is, I strongly suggest researching the organizations to find the one that is right for you. Assistance Dog International is a great place to start.

mine, but I was sad and nervous when it was time to head for home, because I knew my team training friendships and support would no longer be available every day. The friendships I made with classmates would change because we all lived in different states. And even though the trainers were just a phone call or an e-mail away if Yazzen and I needed support, it wasn't the same. Once we graduated, we were on our own. A scary thought—especially since I have never liked change!

Life before Canine Companions and Yazzen was good, but I was dependent on others. Before we became partners, everyday tasks like going to school were very difficult because I'd often find myself stuck in situations where I'd have to wait for someone to come and assist me. An example was my inability to get the outer door of the only accessible restroom on my college campus open. As a result, I'd sometimes be late to class because I'd have to wait for someone to help me out of the room.

When I dropped something, I had to ask for help or move my wheelchair footrests out of the way and then make sure I positioned myself so that I could easily bend over and pick up the item. I say easily, but it wasn't that simple to bend over with my seatbelt fastened without feeling like I was cutting myself in half. If I needed an item out of my reach or if I needed up from my couch, I had to ask for help. But I was used to living my life this way and was okay with it because I didn't know differently. But with Yazzen, life was different. Suddenly I had a friend who could do these things for me, and I didn't have to rely on others because I could rely on Yazzen and myself.

When I needed doors opened, he opened them by tugging on a rope I hooked to the door handle. He pulled on the door until I could wedge the footrests of my chair into it to push it open so that we both could walk through. But physical doors weren't the only thing Yazzen opened for me. He also opened doors to more opportunities for social interaction. Before Yazzen, I was sometimes invisible to my peers and other people. In school and places like the mall, people wouldn't always notice me, so they'd walk in front of me, and if I didn't stop, I'd run the risk of having them land in my lap! At school my peers wouldn't go out of their way to strike up a conversation. After Yazzen, I'd randomly hear people say things like, "You have a beautiful dog." And my peers would initiate conversation with me because I now had this incredibly cool dog.

Even though I had to wait a long time for Yazzen and even though he wasn't my first choice, I wouldn't change a thing. After all, the best things in life are worth the wait, and that was true in this case. Words cannot express how thankful I was for him. I was so glad things happened the way they did because I couldn't imagine another dog in his place.

DEFYING DISABILITY AND
DELIGHTING IN DIVERSITY!

Now that you know more about how Yazzen changed my life, I'd like to share how possessing a positive attitude helped, too. I've never been one to let my CP stand in the way of my goals. And with the life-affirming assistance and love of my family and Yazzen, I overcame obstacles to succeed in ways I never thought possible.

Strength and Determination

From the very moment I was born, on June 28, 1981, God gave me and others around me a lesson in strength and determination. I came into this world two and a half months early; weighed only two pounds, twelve ounces; had a severe brain bleed; and needed tubes to help me breathe. But I was determined to survive. At some point, my brain bleed resolved itself, and I became strong enough to pull out my tubes. When I'd pull them out, the nursing staff would put them back in, only to have me pull them out again. Finally, they got the message and understood I was strong enough to breathe on my own. Even so, I still had to stay in the hospital for almost two months. After that, I went home, and my parents thought everything was fine. Then when I was around two months of age, they realized something might be wrong because when they picked me up, my legs would get stiff, cross at my ankle, and stay crossed. There were other signs too. I wasn't crawling on my hands and knees and I wasn't pulling myself up to stand.

At nine months, doctors were concerned because measurements showed that my head was a little bigger than it should've been. Tests revealed that some excess spinal fluid had built up in my brain. As a result, I had to go back to the hospital for ventriculoperitoneal (or VP) shunt surgery to relieve swelling and excess fluid on my brain. During the surgery, doctors inserted two straw-like flexible tubes or catheters; one went into my brain, and the other extended from behind my right ear down to my stomach. They connected the two catheters, and then they inserted a small pump to the catheter behind my ear, which automatically drained the fluid to my stomach. The doctors made my shunt extra long so that I wouldn't have to go in for repeated surgeries as I grew.

My life verse is Philippians 4:13 (New Living Translation, or NLT), "I can do all things through Christ, who gives me strength," even survive brain surgery. Three months after surgery, doctors diagnosed me with CP. From that point on, my parents knew that their lives, my brother's life, and my life would be different.

Perseverance

Consider it pure joy...whenever you face trials of many kinds,
because you know that the testing of your faith develops
perseverance. Let perseverance finish its work so that you
may be mature and complete, not lacking anything.
—JAMES 1:2-4, NEW INTERNATIONAL VERSION (NIV)

When I was ready to start kindergarten in 1986, I was sent to a "special" school because my public school was, in their words, "not equipped" to handle a child like me. My parents didn't know about the Education of Handicapped Children Act of 1975, which gave children with disabilities the right to a free, appropriate public education, just like other children. And even though my parents tried to fight the school, they were told they had no choice but to bus me an hour and a half away from home to attend another school.

This school was not a fun place. I'd spend all day in a single classroom with around nine other students with disabilities, and I was one of only four students who could speak. I was taught math and reading skills from flash cards and *Weekly Reader* magazines, not textbooks.

Not having textbooks to learn from was bad enough, but being disciplined by the principal if we talked to one another during lunch was even worse. We also had artwork torn up and thrown in the trash if we didn't color things the way the teacher thought they should be colored. I remember sitting in art class and being asked to color a picture of a beet. I began coloring my picture green for the beet greens and red for the body of the vegetable. When I proudly showed my picture to the teacher, he crumpled it up and threw it in the trash because "a beet does not look like this."

The only positive thing about this school was that I became friends with Katie and Sarah. I don't know if it was because of our common bond of CP or if it was because we were the only ones in the class who could communicate, but whatever the reason, we became best friends. We were so close that we did everything together, and we nicknamed ourselves the Three

Musketeers. I wanted to stay with them forever, but my parents had other plans for my life.

After seeing what my school day was like during a tour, my parents knew they had to fight to get me in school back home if I was going to have any hope of a future. So when the Individuals with Disabilities Education Act passed in 1990, my parents decided to try and enroll me in my home school district again. This time, when they met to discuss my placement with administrators, my parents were more educated about the law and they had people like my pediatrician and my future itinerant teacher, who supported their belief that I could be successful.[4] As a result, I finally returned to public school in the fourth grade, at the age of nine, but I wasn't functioning at grade level in math or reading. I couldn't read the word "island," and it took me getting an F in both subjects before the school's academic team would agree to place me in the learning disability (LD) classroom. There, the teachers provided more individualized instruction to address my reading comprehension difficulties and my inability to understand basic math concepts. I wasn't in the LD classroom very long for reading, but math was another story. For some reason, my brain just had difficulty grasping basic math, and it still does.

Unfortunately, my academic placement wasn't the only hurdle my family faced. We had to advocate for the construction of the ramps so that I could gain entry into the building, and we had to fight for accessible bathrooms at not only the elementary school but also the middle school and high school. We also dealt with administrators who wanted to make me wear a helmet when I was walking the hallways. They also wanted to have me stand on a carpet sample during dodgeball in gym, making me an easy target.

---

4 Author's note: An itinerant teacher is a special education teacher who provides mainstreamed students with services so that educational progress can be enhanced. My teacher helped my parents and me advocate for accommodations with teachers and administrators, so my parents didn't always have to be the bad guys. When I first came back, she helped me explain to my peers how CP affects me. She had them get in wheelchairs and try to pick up a dropped pencil without getting up. She also took away their ability to use their dominant hand, and they had to try to write and pick things up with their non-dominant hand. These exercises, coupled with giving my peers the opportunity to ask questions, helped me be more accepted by them.

I'd like to think that they were doing these things out of concern for my safety, but in reality, they were afraid of being sued if something happened to me. You see, I was the first student with a disability to attend school in my district. The administrators didn't know any better, but what they failed to realize was that I was the same as any other child. I just happened to have a body that was uniquely able, not disabled. The things they wanted me to do weren't going to help my peers accept me. They would only reinforce our differences.

As a result, I had to educate people and let them know I wasn't a porcelain doll. I wouldn't break if I fell or was hit by a ball. Looking back, I am thankful for every trial I've ever had to face because they built up my character and helped me become the woman I am today.

I've always worked very hard to prove to others that I'm a person who is very capable of living a productive life despite having CP. When someone would tell me, "You can't," I'd work twice as hard to prove that I could. For example, when I wanted to pull myself out of LD for math in eighth grade because I was tired of learning the same concepts, administrators tried to tell me I couldn't do it, but my parent's and the math teacher let me try. And I earned some of the highest grades in the class!

Due to the support and acceptance of my family and friends, I don't see myself as a person with a disability because I choose not to. I can remember shopping with my mom, and when we stopped to eat lunch, I turned to her and said, "Man, I didn't realize how tired I was until we sat down." She laughed and said, "You've been sitting!"

I've always seen myself as the same as anybody else, and I've always tried to stay focused on my capabilities. If I wanted to do something, I did it. For example, in middle school, I decided that I wanted to be a cheerleader after seeing a news story about a girl in a manual chair cheering on the sidelines of her school's basketball court. I knew then that I could do it too. And middle school was the perfect time for me to try because we didn't have try-outs, so I knew I'd have a spot on the squad. Being a cheerleader was fun. And during my two years on the squad, the girls included me and made me feel like I was part of the team. I can remember this one cheer we did for a jump ball, "J-u-m-p, jump Tigers, jump." Well, on jump Tigers jump, one cheerleader would get behind the other, and lift her slightly up off the ground. Obviously, I couldn't do this, but one of the girls decided that she'd use the handlebars on the back of my chair to lift herself up when it came to that part, so that I'd be included. As much fun as I had cheerleading, I knew that I didn't want to be a cheerleader in high school. But I was thankful for the opportunity I had to be one of the girls.

Yes, CP is part of who I am. I celebrate and sometimes curse it, especially when my limitations seem to stand in the way of accomplishing my goals. However, I refuse to let it define me, and I refuse to let it get in my way. To this day, when someone or something stands in the way of me and my goals, I become like the bull who charges the red flag of its matador. When faced with a challenge, I don't back down from it. Instead, I rise to meet it, and I work hard to try and conquer it. Just ask my former physical therapy assistant who ended up bald, not once but twice, because he bet that I couldn't walk a certain number of laps around their great room.

If you're going through tough times and things seem impossible, don't give up on yourself. Find something to believe in or someone you can confide in and draw your strength from. Most importantly, believe in yourself, and know you already have what it takes to overcome your challenges and accomplish your goals. It will be hard, but you can do it!

Acceptance

People have often commented on how I always have the biggest smile on my face no matter what I seem to be going through. It would be so easy for me to have a bad attitude and be down, and sometimes I get that way. However, most of the time I choose to be happy. I choose to have that smile on my face because the alternative gets me nowhere. As my friend Lisa says, "Happiness comes from within. It is your interpretation of your reality, the people you surround yourself with, and your acceptance of God's plan for your life." (Marn 2015) Therefore, I can be happy because I know He has a plan for me, and I have people in my life who believe in me and support me. Therefore, it's easier to deal with my CP and everything that comes with it.

Self-Acceptance

If you have ever felt different, like you do not fit in or belong, you are not alone. I, too, have felt this way, and sometimes I still do. However, if you're dealing with feeling different, you need to know that being different is what makes you unique. Don't worry about trying to fit in or be normal. You are perfect just the way you are. As Maya Angelou said, "If you are always trying to be normal, you will never know how amazing you can be." (Angelou 2015) Realize that no one is normal. Everyone has challenges or differences that should be embraced, not seen as a mistake or something that needs to change. I believe we are all exactly who we're meant to be. There are *no* mistakes.[5]

Acceptance from Others

When I was growing up, friendships didn't come easy because I wasn't able to go to school with my peers. My mom put me in Brownies with the hope that I'd develop relationships. Being a fellow Brownie helped, but I never felt like I fit in.

_____

5 Author's note: See Psalm 139:13-14 and Exodus 4:11, NIV.

When I came back to my home school district, my peers would initially be my friends, but after a while they would begin to ignore me or exclude me. I recall being out on the playground one day. One minute I was playing with some friends and everything was fine, and the next, they had left me sitting there alone in the gravel while they went to play with someone or something else. At that moment, I felt sad, rejected, and embarrassed because my one-to-one aide had to rescue me from the quicksand like gravel. The more I tried to move, the more the wheels of my manual chair, which I used at the time, got stuck, and I couldn't free myself. When things like this happened, I was glad Katie, Sarah, and I had stayed friends. They were back at their home district for school too, and I knew they might be the only ones who could understand what I was going through. We were always there for one another, and we could count on one another for support when we couldn't count on our other friends. Katie, Sarah, and I stayed friends through high school. Though we grew apart during college, I would like to reconnect now.

Even though most of the experiences I remember with my friends and peers were negative, there were some positive experiences too. Like my first slumber party, my time as cheerleader, and my high school dances. I especially remember my junior prom in May of 1999.[6]

That night I was being hounded by a photographer and reporter from the Beacon Newspaper, who were finishing up a story about my experiences with inclusion, titled "Class Act| Born with Cerebral Palsy, Amy Chally Finds Success in Mainstream Education." Well, my upperclassman friends could tell that I was getting rather annoyed by the presence of the reporter and photographer who wouldn't leave. So they created a circle around me and danced with me so that the photographer couldn't get any more shots. During that moment, I felt more included than I ever had. A lot of the girls left their dates to dance with me for a while, and they made sure I had a good time.

Their actions that night meant a lot, and I wish I would've had more of an opportunity to have a relationship with those girls outside of school. Even

---

6 Author's note: I always went to my homecomings and proms without a date. And despite the fact that I couldn't really dance, I always had fun. Don't let the possibility of not having a date or not being able to dance, discourage you from fun.

though I did have some good relationships with my peers, I didn't have many friends, and I never felt fully accepted by them.

If you are having a hard time developing friendships with your peers, understand that difficulty with friendships is a normal part of growing up. But trust me when I tell you that as you get older, friendships become easier. The friends I have now accept me for who I am, and they don't treat me as if I'm different. My friends realize that I like the same things they do. They know that I love life, I enjoy water skiing, and I like to try new things.[7] Together my friends and I have gone to concerts, gotten our nails done, gone on girls' trips, and just hung out. I don't get to see them much any more because they are busy with their lives, but I miss them, and I hope they know how much their friendship still means to me. They gave me the greatest gift: acceptance. True acceptance means so much and is so important to those who are different.

So if you see others who are different from you, don't be mean. Don't ignore them or exclude them. Be their friend, include them in activities, talk to them, and get to know them. Don't be afraid to ask them questions, even if your questions are about what makes them different. Being their friend could be the best thing you do, not only for them but for you, too. I always like it when people ask me questions to get to know me and better understand my CP. I would rather have someone ask how I do something, or if I need help, rather than have someone assume I can't do a task and automatically help me.

In fact, one thing I love to do is give community presentations where I tell people about my condition, CCI, and then demonstrate how my dog helps me. Yazzen and I gave many of these presentations throughout our partnership, and one place we loved to visit was a school. When we got to the question-and-answer session, each time without fail, some little boy would bravely raise his hand and ask, "How do you go to the bathroom?" On our last visit to a school I was asked that question and I responded by telling him that I go to the bathroom just like any other person but with a few differences. For instance, I might need the door opened for me, and I have to use a handicapped accessible stall

---

7 Author's note: I water ski using a sit ski—a bucket seat attached to a single ski with outriggers or extra supports on each side. I've never experienced anything more freeing! Go to: youtube.com / watch?v=hAC_6y0p12E to see me in action. The next new thing I'd like to try is zip-lining.

that's big enough for my wheelchair and equipped with grab bars for me to hold on to. Otherwise I'd fall.

Students also wanted to know how I sleep, get myself dressed, and if I could cook, clean, do the laundry, or drive a car. I shared that I sleep just like anyone else would except my bedroom is downstairs on my house's main floor. And although it's not easy, I can get myself in and out of bed. I can also bathe myself and get myself dressed, including pulling up my pants, with the use of the grab bar in my bathroom. I prefer to have assistance putting on my socks and shoes, not only because I can't tie the laces, but also because when I put them on myself, I have to bend over in my chair. The blood goes rushing to my head, and I turn beet red!

Due to fine motor or small movement limitations, dexterity issues, and my high muscle tone, I don't have very good use of my left hand.[8] As a result, I am predominantly right-handed. Therefore, I can't cook or cut my food with a knife and a fork, so somebody usually prepares my meals and cuts my food. If someone makes my meals, I can get them out of the refrigerator, warm them up in the microwave, get out any condiments necessary, cut my food with my one-handed rocker knife if needed, and eat. I'm also capable of getting my snacks and making simple things like a sandwich or a cup of hot tea if I want it. Except for some light dusting and scrubbing my bathroom sink, I cannot clean, make my bed, or wash and fold my clothes. But I can strip my bedding, and my dog can help me tug my dirty laundry to the basement stairs to be taken down and washed.

While some people with physical disabilities can drive a car with the help of hand gears and other adaptive equipment, that isn't the case for me. Due to my CP, I have a tendency to jump at loud, unexpected sounds like sirens. I also can't track movement with my eyes without moving my head, too. As a result, it wouldn't be safe for me to drive. But I can utilize public transportation, Pace Dial-a-Ride, or Paratransit to help me get where I need or want to go.[9]

---

8 Author's note: Dexterity refers to a person's ability to use their hands. A person with good dexterity can get their fingers and hands to work together to complete fine tasks.

9 Author's note: Pace Paratransit is a service required by the ADA for persons with disabilities whose condition prevents them from using the public trains or buses for some or all of their travel.

Faith

I don't understand why God allows certain things to happen, but at least in my case, I believe things happened for a reason. I believe I am supposed to use my academic, personal, and professional struggles and triumphs to educate others and to be an inspiration, an encouragement, and a beacon of hope for other people with disabilities and their families. It's my heart's desire to help individuals become all they can be, no matter their challenges.

I sometimes wish that I could dance or even walk on this earth without the aid of a walker. However, I wouldn't want to change anything, except maybe my inability to drive, as that obstacle is an ongoing source of extreme frustration. But I know God had a plan when I was born with CP, when I went to the "special" school, and when I received Yazzen. And He has a plan for me today. To be honest, much of the time I struggle to understand His plan. But Proverbs 3:5-6 NIV says, "Trust in the Lord with all your heart; and lean not unto your own understanding." So I try to remember that God doesn't give someone more than he or she can handle—He's in control, and He has promised me a future that will prosper me, not harm me, and give me hope (Jeremiah 29:11, NIV).

I overcame my academic challenges and went on to earn a Master's degree in social work, graduated with honors, and became a licensed social worker. Most of the time, social work jobs require a valid driver's license, CPR certification, and the ability to speak Spanish and to conduct home visits. These requirements make it difficult, but not impossible, for me to find a job in my field. However, one thing I've learned is that no matter what difficulty I face, I'll get through it, and I'll come away from it being a stronger, better person.

I dream of the day when I can wake up, go to work at a stable job, and enjoy what I'm doing so much that it doesn't even feel like I'm working. I dream of a day when I can save up money to rent my own place, without being fearful of losing my personal assistant services through the state. I even dream of meeting Mr. Right someday, getting married, and becoming a mom. But for now, those dreams will have to wait, because I was laid off in June of 2015. So once again, I have to figure out how He wants to use me and my degree, but I know that with God by my side, nothing is impossible; He gives me strength and makes my way perfect (Luke 1:37 NLT; Psalm 18:32 NLT). Therefore, I know that in His time, I'll overcome my obstacles to employment, and I have faith that my life will work out the way it's meant to.

So have faith, my friend, and remember that no matter what trials you face, you are strong, and you will be okay. Always remember this: you are never alone. There are people who believe in you and love you. And God believes in you and loves you.

EPILOGUE

In May 2014, Yazzen's mast cell cancer returned and the grapefruit-sized tumor was under his right front leg. Because of the size and location of the tumor, he was unable to work, and while he was sick, I was forced to experience what my life would be like without him. I was dependent on other people again, and I didn't like living that way. Sadly, Yazzen never got to come back to work for me. Instead, he retired and lived with my parents and me as our pet, which gave him a lot of time to play fetch. I'm sorry to say that Yazzen lost his battle with cancer, and he passed away in July 2014. This time around the disease was too advanced, and no surgery or treatment would cure him for good. I was so sad when he died because our relationship went way beyond that of a woman and her dog. The day we said our good-byes I wrote this letter to him:

July 7, 2014

My boy,

Today my heart breaks because I had to let you go. I'll miss you, my boy, and I'll hate not having you here with me, but you'll always be with me because you have my heart, and I have our memories. When I first got you from Canine Companions for Independence nearly nine years ago, I was skeptical. You were so stubborn, and you refused to wag your tail. When I look back, it was fitting that a stubborn woman would get matched with a dog who was just as stubborn. During team training, our bond strengthened, and before long your stubborn streak dissipated and your tail began to wag. I'll miss your wagging tail.

You eventually became the heart and soul of Team Chally. I'll miss the way you worked so hard to please me and how, when you didn't know what I wanted, you'd bring me everything you could get your mouth on, just because you wanted to see me happy. As a result, you'd make me smile, laugh, or both. You had a way of making me smile or laugh a lot! Thank you for that and thank you for giving your life to make every day of my life better. You've been a true godsend, a truly unexpected and needed gift from above. He broke the mold when He made you. You're one in a billion, not just a million! Thank you for being my lifeline to independence, my friend, my constant companion, the one who never left my side. Thank you for being the best brother to two little dogs who will miss you dearly, too.

My boy, I'd give anything to keep you here with me, but that'd be selfish, and you deserve better than that. You deserve a life free of sickness and pain. So sleep well, my boy, rest in peace, knowing that you've done a great job, knowing that I'll love you forever, and I'll be "OK." [10]

All my love,
Amy

---

10 Author's note: Because of who Yazzen was and because of what he did for my life, I knew without a doubt that I'd need and want another team member. So in August 2014, my mom and I headed back to team training, and I received Portland II, the newest member of Team Chally! I don't want to tell you any more than that because we may write a sequel. However, if you can't wait to see what we have been up to lately, you can spoil the surprise and go to TeamChally.com or Facebook.com/team.chally!

References

Angelou, Maya. *Goodreads*. Accessed February 15, 2015. http://www.goodreads. com/quotes/700564-if-you-are-always-trying-to-be-normal-you-will.

Birth Village. Accessed March 29, 2014. www.birthvillage.com/Name/Yasin.

Canine Companions for Independence. 2013. "Breeding Program." Accessed March 29, 2014. http://www.cci.org/site/c.cdKGIRNqEmG/b.4011113/k. A434/Breeding_Program.htm.

_____. 2013. "Canine Companions Assistance Dogs." Accessed March 29, 2014. http://www.cci.org/site/c.cdKGIRNqEmG/b.4011017/k.2900/ Canine_Companions_Assistance_Dogs.htm.

_____. 2013. "Puppy Raising Program." Accessed March 29, 2014. http:// www.cci.org/site/c.cdKGIRNqEmG/b.4011029/k.6CF1/Puppy_Raising_ Program.htm.

_____. 2013. "The Application Process." Accessed March 29, 2014. http:// www.cci.org/site/c.cdKGIRNqEmG/b.4011037/k.463/Application_ Process.htm.

_____. 2013. "The Experience." Accessed March 29, 2014. http://www.cci. org/site/c.cdKGIRNqEmG/b.4011035/k.8E5F/The_Experience.htm.

_____. 2012. "The Puppy Name Game." Accessed March 29, 2014. http:// blog.cci.org/2012/09/21/the-puppy-name-game/.

_____.2013. "Training Assistance Dogs." Accessed March 29, 2014. http://www. cci.org/site/c.cdKGIRNqEmG/b.4011115/k.65BA/Training_assistance_ dogs.htm.

Doe, Carol. 2014. "Carol's Journey with CCI Puppy—'Helper II.'" Last Modified January 10, 2014. Accessed March 29, 2014. http://helper2012.blogspot.com/.

Cortez, Linda. 2004. *South Bay Champions Newsletter.* November/December Issue. Accessed March 29, 2014. http://www.sbchamps.org/Newsletters/jan04nl.pdf.

Fatka, Eric. Interview by Amy Chally. December 8, 2012. Personal Communication.

First-Names-Meanings; Baby Names Numerology. Accessed March 29, 2014. http://www.first-names-meanings.com/names/name-YASSINE.html; http://www.babynamesnumerology.com/meaning-of-yazan.html.

Larin, Daniel, and Linda Cortez. Interview by Amy Chally. August 23, 2013. Personal Communication.

Marn, Lisa. 2015. Facebook Post. Last modified September 18, 2015. Accessed October 2015. www.facebook.com.

O'Connell, Lisa. Interview by Amy Chally. July 9, 2012. Personal Communication.

CPSIA information can be obtained
at www.ICGtesting.com
Printed in the USA
LVOW10s0024200617

538683LV00012B/778/P